History

The Unofficial History of the Paddington Bear

By Jennifer Warner

BookCaps™ Study Guides

www.bookcaps.com

© 2014. All Rights Reserved.

Cover Image © Hedgehog - Fotolia.com

Table of Contents

ABOUT LIFECAPS 3

THE UNOFFICIAL HISTORY OF PADDINGTON BEAR 4

WORKS CITED 100

About LifeCaps

HistoryCaps is an imprint of BookCaps™ Study Guides. With each book, a brief period of history is recapped. We publish a wide array of topics (from baseball and music to science and philosophy), so check our growing catalogue regularly (**www.bookcaps.com**) to see our newest books.

The Unofficial History of Paddington Bear

In this world of superheroes, bells-and-whistles gadgetry, and mind blowing techno-magic, isn't it amazing that the elements of a simple story can still capture the imagination and appeal to the senses? Well, maybe not just any simple story, but a well written one that extols the very best in human nature while at the same time exposing weaknesses and meeting problems head on, with characters who are accessible, relatable, and believable, is sure to find its place in the annals of classic, timeless literature. This is the case with the easy, fluid stories penned by Michael Bond for more than fifty years, featuring the irresistible, furry little stowaway who came to be known as Paddington Bear. His journey from Darkest Peru is rivaled only by his journey from the depths of Michael Bond's imagination, which goes something like this…

Thomas Michael Bond was born on January 13, 1926 in Berkshire, England to Norman and Frances Bond, an only child. His father was a post office administrator who was transferred to Reading when Michael was just an infant. As a child growing up fairly poor, he enjoyed the usual activities of the day—bicycling, cricket, ice skating. His favorite toy was reportedly his Meccano Set, also called an erector set, because it taught him to use his hands and imagination. He also put his imagination to use in the books he read. Both parents were avid readers, and books were practically a part of the furniture in their house. Michael read Rupert Bear, Grimms' fairy tales, Hans Christian Andersen, and a favorite, Wyss's *The Swiss Family Robinson*. He also found adventure in the writings of W. E. Johns in the *Biggles* series about an adventuresome pilot by the same name, and Sapper's *Bulldog Drummond*, dubbed a "detective, patriot, hero, and gentleman" in the 1920 novel. The weekly stories for boys published in the *Magnet*, mostly written by Charles Hamilton (usually under the pen name of Frank Richards), and featuring the exploits of a group of schoolboys and their ringleader Billy Bunter also tickled his fancy.

The town of Reading during the time of Bond's childhood had two theatres, three cinemas, and boasted a jail where Oscar Wilde was once locked in cell #33. The first "talkie" to play there was Al Jolson's *The Singing Fool*. Nearly everything was delivered to homes in those days—milk, bread, vegetables—and other things were available at Mrs. Robins' corner shop near the Bond family home. While Michael was intrigued by words at a very early age, his career aspirations vacillated between being an engine driver, a lion tamer, or a tightrope walker, no doubt influenced by the town's train system and the appearance of the circus periodically.

A favorite pastime of Michael's as a child was to take off with his best friend Tim on long bicycle trips, sometimes as many as a hundred miles per day, carrying camping equipment and provisions and once remarking, "The world was our oyster." Likewise, the cinema in those days, which cost one shilling and ninepence for a double feature and all the extras, introduced him to cartoons, newsreels, and unforgettable characters from the Three Stooges to Claudette Colbert and Deanna Durbin, for whom he expressed a deep love at an early age. Michael also took a great interest in building radio sets and amplifiers. He remembers fondly playing with Ebonite, pieces of wire, valves, and large coils. His fascination with radios would play a part in his acquiring one of his first jobs, with the BBC Radio.

His schooling options, Bond reported, were like "pot luck; a matter of one's family living in a certain place at a certain time." He reportedly attended Catholic school, not because the family was Catholic, but because his mother fancied the color of the blazers. Bond described English schools of the time, and his in particular, as providing him "an invaluable grounding in the fact that life is basically unfair," and that they prepared him for the worst in life, noting, "It's rather like serving a prison sentence before you commit the crime."[1] Common forms of punishment included caning and ear tweaking. He fairly despised school, and often sought ways to miss it by faking illnesses and the like. He finally left altogether when he was fourteen, feeling that he was somewhat of a disappointment to his family, but thinking that he would someday, somehow make up for it. One of his last report cards stated, "Bond suffers from a distorted sense of humour."[2]

---

[1] Bond, p. 40.

[2] Bond, p. 58.

After leaving school at the age of fourteen, Bond went to work at a solicitor's office, thinking that he might want to pursue such a career for himself. However, he was quite convinced by the experience that he preferred a career that was not so boring and inconsequential. He came to this realization after one of the partners retired from the firm, never to be seen or heard from again, as though he had never existed. This prompted him to answer an advertisement stating simply, "Wanted: Someone interested in radio." He indeed got the job as a trainee engineer for the local BBC radio transmitter, and his career in mass media was born.

With Bond's penchant for animal characters, one might think he had been a pet lover as a child. As it happened, he recalled having three guinea pigs which he named Pip, Squeak, and Wilfred (after a popular cartoon series back then), but felt quite disappointed and betrayed when one of them up and gave birth to a litter of babies. He was never sure which of the trio was the culprit, but from then on decided to devote his attention wholly to his dog Binkie, who remained his best friend until he left home.

In January 1943, on his seventeenth birthday, Michael volunteered for the Royal Air Force and went to Perth for flight training. However, when it became clear that he would be violently sick each time he went up in an airplane, the RAF sent him back to England with the option of working in the coal mines or transferring to the Army. He chose the Army, joining the Middlesex Regiment in 1944 and assuming his first post in Egypt in 1945. Of his Army life, he said, "In between futile fatigues aimed at keeping us occupied—like picking up stones in the desert 'because they made it look untidy,' saluting anything that moved and whitewashing anything that didn't, I sat down one evening and sublimated my desires of the flesh by writing a short story set in a sleazy Cairo bar. I called it 'Captain Hazel's Piece of String' and I sent it to a magazine called *London Opinion*."[3] He found that it was accepted when, three months later, he received a check for seven guineas, which no one in Egypt would cash for him.

---

[3] Commire, p.29.

Regardless, he continued writing for this magazine, as well as for *Men Only* and *Manchester Guardian,* though he admits that success as a writer was slow in coming. In those days, to sell one in twelve pieces was considered a good year's work. His hero was Ernest Hemingway. Having heard that Hemingway was being paid $1 per word, he determined to develop a writing style which used a large number of very small words. He left the Army in 1947 and returned to his former radio job, which eventually led him to become a cameraman for the BBC. He worked up the ranks as a cameraman and transferred to the BBC's children's television department, where he worked on the first series of the program *Blue Peter*. Around this time, his writing took a decided turn, and he began writing plays for radio and adapting W. W. Jacobs's short stories for the BBC.

On June 29, 1950, Bond married Brenda Mary Johnson. He admits that he was probably not ready to marry at the time, but after sort of stumbling unwittingly into a marriage proposal, she accepted before he knew it. In 1958, shortly before the first Paddington book was published, their daughter Karen was born. Karen sort of grew up with Paddington and at times it was difficult, sometimes being referred to as Paddington's "sister," and Michael worried that she would struggle to find her own identity. But alas, she managed to grow up more or less unharmed and, as Mrs. Bird might say, with a good head on her shoulders.

Michael and Brenda's marriage ended in the seventies, though they have reportedly remained great friends over the years. For a while, Michael had a romantic relationship with one of his editors, out of which his son Anthony was born in 1977. Shortly after his birth, this relationship also ended. Bond noted, "Eve and I were too opposite in our outlook on life for our relationship to become permanent."[4] Though this was a difficult time for Bond, he threw himself into his work, as writers are apt to do in times of trouble.

---

[4] Bond, p. 203.

In the 1960s, Bond's writing career began to take center stage in his life. Though he had worked up in the ranks to senior cameraman, he began to lose interest in his work with the BBC. His job began to require more and more paperwork, traveling, and supervision of employees, which distracted him from his real love—filming. Even the excitement of filming began to wane with the advent of video recording, and though he spoke of his time with the BBC as "enormously enriching," he left the job in 1965 to pursue his writing career full-time. He also formed Paddington and Company Films, Ltd. (later shortened to Paddington and Company), opening a London office where he planned to both write and manage the growing Paddington Bear merchandising market.

Managing the commercialization of Paddington, however, proved more daunting than he could have imagined, and he eventually hired Nicholas Durbridge to take the helm. The work involved granting licenses, chasing down pirates, overseeing safety and quality issues related to the licensed products, answering correspondence, pursuing litigation for copyright infringements, and generally protecting Paddington's image. In 1978, the office moved from Beak Street to 22 Crawford Place, where they renovated on old ramshackle building to house the offices upstairs, and a "Paddington and Friends" retail shop on the ground floor. The shop sells the current Paddington Bear products as well as the lines that emerged from Bond's other storybook characters, including Olga da Polga and The Herbs. Bond's daughter Karen assumed the role of Managing Director of Paddington and Company in the mid-1980s.

In 1976, Stephen Durbridge, brother of Nicholas, joined Harvey Unna's literary agency and brought with him his assistant, Sue. This lady immediately captured Michael's attention, and he invited her to go with him to the Paddington play that was being staged in a London suburb. The play turned out to be a bomb, but the relationship grew and they moved in together, eventually marrying in 1981. Sue accompanied Michael and Graham Clutterbuck on several of their trips. One, a book tour of Australia and New Zealand in 1979, proved to be very harrowing, at times demoralizing, and not an especially high point in Bond's career. He much preferred traveling in France, claiming that he is most inspired there, and in fact his time in Paris likely played a huge part in one of his most prized projects.

While Bond is best known for his role in the Paddington Bear dynasty, he has penned many other children's books. A series of four books featuring Thursday the Mouse was written from 1966 through 1971. Thursday was a whimsical mouse who managed a daring escape from the Home for Waif-Mice, a sort of mouse orphanage. Olga da Polga, a tall tale telling guinea pig character who is comfortable with adventure and challenges only in the context of her own fantastic stories, stars in six chapter books and eight picture books that Bond wrote beginning in the early 1970s. Bond even created an armadillo character in the 1980s named J. D. Polson, who hails from Texas since, as everyone knows, there are no armadillos in England. The funny little guy somehow finds himself as none other than the President of the United States in the first book! The Olga books had a fair amount of success, but nothing compared to that of her cousin Paddington.

Michael was looking for a change from children's writing in the early 1980s, and set out to do a detective series for adults. Monsieur Pamplemousse, the first in the series, was published in 1983. The title character, a detective who had taken "early" retirement from the Paris Sûreté (police force), was prone to accidents and "landing himself in compromising situations." After his retirement he became a food inspector traveling all over France with a special knack for recognizing "nefarious goings-on."[5] Bond would go on to write twenty-one titles for the Monsieur Pamplemousse series.

In 1987, Bond published *The Pleasures of Paris*. He loved France from the first time he visited the country, and his love of French food, wine, and photography led him to do the book. Bond did all of the writing and the illustrations in this book. His writing style is self-described: "I work solidly, weekends included. I tend to wake up early, sometimes I start work at four in the morning. But I enjoy it…I get depressed about a third of the way through a book, when I can't really see the end, but by the time I'm three-quarters of the way through and know how it will finish I start to think about the next one."[6]

---

[5] Bond, p. 230.

[6] Commire, p. 29.

Somewhere, somehow in the midst of the busy life of this husband, father, cameraman, writer, a series of events unfolded from which a lovable little creature would emerge. Some would call it fate, others happenstance, but the fact remains that a bear was born and the rest, as they say, is history. How *did* this furry phenomenon come about?

It all started with a missed bus. To think that such a mundane and annoying event could be the catalyst that spurs an action to change a person's very life path is almost staggering, but that is exactly what happened to Michael Bond on Christmas Eve of 1956, no less. After realizing the No. 12 bus had left without him, he ventured into a London department store to get out of the rain and pass the time, and wandered into the toy department where he was drawn to the sight of a lone teddy bear on a shelf. Whether it was the Christmas spirit or his whimsical nature, he found himself picking it up and purchasing it. He had already completed his Christmas shopping for his wife Brenda, and he had no children at the time, but he simply could not allow the poor guy to languish on a store shelf, alone, throughout the holidays. Determining to add it to Brenda's stocking, he and the bear left the store and caught the next bus home.

The cute bear was a big hit with Brenda and soon was adopted as a full member of the family. He became simply "Bear" until a more proper name could be decided upon. Very quickly, Bear was set up with his own tiny bed and acquired a duffle coat, small suitcase, and a green hat and scarf knitted by Brenda. To Michael Bond, names were important and should be carefully thought out, so as to be both fitting and meaningful. The name "Paddington" was finally chosen, as the Bonds lived near the district in London and the train station by the same name.

One day soon after the bear came to live with them, Bond set out to write a story, "just to get his brain working,"[7] looking to the bear for inspiration. He was pondering what might have happened if his "inspiration" had made his way to Paddington Station all the way across the world by himself. In the back of his mind, he pictured the newsreels he had seen during the war, of trainloads of tearful children being evacuated from London. Each child wore an attached label and carried a small suitcase.

---

[7] Ash, p. 16.

What followed was a story in which the orphan bear was sent to England from Darkest Africa by his Aunt Lucy, who was elderly and had to move into a home for retired bears. His aunt carefully prepared him for the trip by teaching him to speak English, packing marmalade in his suitcase to eat on his journey, and attaching a label to his collar stating, "Please look after this bear. Thank you." He arrived as a stowaway on Paddington Station, where he was found by Mr. and Mrs. Brown, who quickly adopted and took him home to live with them and their two children. The bear's label and small, tattered suitcase, inspired by London's young evacuees so many years ago, made him irresistible to the Browns.

Michael wrote the first chapter before lunch that day, and a chapter per day after that, declaring it finished after eight days. Never intending it for publication, he did let Brenda read it and he evaluated the stories by the number of laughs they evoked. Apparently the laughs were frequent and genuine, because he was strongly encouraged to submit the "totally unpremeditated book"[8] to his agent for possible publication.

---

[8] Bond, p. 154.

Bond's literary agent, Harvey Unna, responded that he liked the book but cautioned him that the children's market was very competitive; nevertheless, Unna encouraged him to do a rewrite. In the second round, Harvey and his "spies" pointed out that there were, in fact, no bears then living in Darkest Africa or any other part of Africa for that matter, and advised changing Paddington's country of origin. After doing a more thorough job of researching the subject, "Darkest Peru" was decided on and approved. Unna then submitted the book to several publishing houses and it was accepted by Collins, where editor Barbara Ker Wilson was quite taken with it.

As there were no illustrations with the manuscript, Wilson recommended illustrator Peggy Fortnum, who quickly sketched approximately fifty black and white drawings of Paddington in his various surroundings and situations. Bond approved, and the book went to print, including over thirty of Fortnum's drawings. *A Bear Called Paddington* was published in hardback on October 13, 1958. It quickly received favorable reviews and was sold out before Christmas 1958.

Over the next year, the book became a bestseller and was published in several other countries. It was first published in the United States in September of 1960 by Houghton Mifflin and sold for $2.50. The popular reviewer E. W. Richter placed the book on a par with Dr. Seuss, calling it "classic." When Bond was later asked to explain Paddington's quick success, he commented, "If you're totally honest with yourself, there's a little voice inside you that tells you if something is right or if it's wrong—and you ignore it at your peril. I didn't have any little voices with Paddington. If I had to do it again, I wouldn't change anything. It's easy to say after the event, but I always had a feeling that Paddington would be successful."[9]

---

[9] Ash, p. 28.

Bond is credited with not oversimplifying the language in his books and putting together the perfect "cast of characters." The Brown family is endearing, immediately finding a soft spot for Paddington Bear, and this is balanced by the very firm, sometimes cross, and always omniscient Mrs. Bird. Bond would later admit that the inspiration for Mrs. Bird was part Mary Gordon/ Mrs. Hudson of Sherlock Holmes films, and part childhood friend Tim's Aunt Hetty. Since Paddington Bear was an immigrant, another immigrant was added to the mix in the form of Mr. Gruber, with Paddington thereby creating a winning duo, both equally baffled by the nuances of British life but ever understanding of each other. Bond later revealed that Mr. Gruber's character was modeled after his agent Harvey Unna, who escaped Germany just before the war. Another character, the Browns' neighbor Mr. Curry, was known to be a grouch and had a way of triggering some of Paddington's "adventures." Mr. Curry is representative of the grouch in everyone's life. The writing was unapologetically patterned after the *Magnet* stories by Frank Richards that Bond devoured as a child. Richards, according to Bond, "respected his audience. He never wrote down and he never preached."[10]

---

[10] Bond, p. 157.

Through the years, many questions have been raised about the story's characters and background, some of which were never answered in the books. One of the more popular queries was "What happened to Paddington's uncle?" In order to put this question to bed once and for all, the *Observer* held a competition, inviting children to submit their own theories. One child explained that the uncle had been kidnapped and forced to work in the dreaded marmalade mines, and in fact, Paddington Bear looks for a message from him whenever a new jar is opened! Bond's own theory suggests that he became filthy rich selling cocoa to silver prospectors and retired. But then, what would he know about it?

Another popular question is "What is Paddington's real (Peruvian) name?" It is not answered in the books, except for Paddington to say he only has "a Peruvian one which no one can understand," in the first novel. The absence of an answer wasn't problematic until the books were being published in Japan, where Paddington Bear would eventually have a cult-like following. The Japanese had the audacity to refuse Paddington's own answer and insist on knowing the bear's Peruvian name. With Bond being known as a very persnickety name-chooser, work came to a standstill while he contacted his South American cousin, living in New York at the time, and put her up to the task of finding a proper Peruvian name. Eventually the name "Pastuzo" was decided upon, meaning "slow-moving and solid."[11]

---

[11] Ash, p. 30.

Some also have asked through the years, "Why marmalade?" There is no doubt that this tasty sweet plays an enormous role in Paddington's life. Traditionally, bears are believed to be lovers of honey, so where did the idea of marmalade originate? Michael admits that he wanted to use something a little more interesting than the customary honey, and it just happens that he has a special affinity for marmalade himself, so it seemed the logical choice. Besides, marmalade is a very British commodity, and despite his Peruvian origin, Paddington is actually quite a British bear.

Is the character of Paddington Bear patterned after a real person? Many would try to say that Paddington *is* Michael Bond, an assertion that he vehemently denies. The little guy does seem to have some similar qualities to Norman Bond, Michael's father; for example, Norman Bond was always excited at the prospect of a do-it-yourself project around the house, but nearly always proved totally inept in the execution of said project. Bond's father once exploded their kitchen, while simply trying to follow his wife's instructions to warm up the oven. Additionally, some of Paddington's activities and settings seem to come from Bond's family life, with locations such as Paddington Station, Notting Hill, and Portobello Road being places where they could frequently be found.

Paddington's undertakings often seemed to mimic the activities of Bond's daughter Karen, as she explored such things as waterskiing and horseback riding while growing up. The story of Paddington being injured and going into the hospital was at least partly inspired by his daughter Karen's experiences as a child. She was born with a congenital hip dislocation, and spent long periods of time in the hospital at an early age. The experience was often scary for her and very difficult for her parents, as in those days parents were not permitted to stay with their children and could only see them during visiting hours. Paddington's hospital stay was not altogether unpleasant, and was meant to both inform and assure children facing sickness, injury, or the prospect of an overnight stay in a hospital. Oftentimes, some of Bond's own interests and activities would also pop up in a story, i.e., photography, cooking, or going to the dentist.

Bond may say that he is not Paddington, but he is also quick to point out that he wouldn't mind it at times. "The bear has a very good life, well organized with no obvious worries, and though he is far from lazy, he does not work…Paddington's undeniable strength of character enables him to win through no matter what…he says exactly what he thinks without hesitation…and he always comes out on top."[12] Indeed, if Michael meets with a challenge in his everyday life, he may very well back down meekly, but once he writes Paddington into the same situation, you can be sure he will stand his ground and find a way to prevail. The stories are very realistically based in everyday settings and ordinary activities, but with Paddington there is always the absence of ordinariness. His world is safe and secure, with few pervasions of modern marvels, making the stories timeless and classic. What you have, then, is "a unique creature capable of wreaking havoc in an otherwise mundane world."[13]

---

[12] Ash, p. 40-41.

[13] Ash, p. 43.

It has been suggested that the reason for Paddington's very thorough and immediate success is plain and simple: he's a bear. Kids have been loving teddy bears for generations, and for many years bears have made memorable characters. There is Br'er Bear from the *Uncle Remus* stories, the lovable Winnie the Pooh, the adventuresome Rupert, the smarter-than-the-average-bear Yogi, and those mysterious bears of *Goldilocks* fame, to name a few. Bond himself has commented that a bear makes such a better companion than, say, a doll, because "dolls only wonder about what they will wear, while you never know what a bear is thinking." Of course, Paddington himself is a self-proclaimed rarity, having been the only one of this revered group to hail from Darkest Peru, which surely gives him a slight edge over these more common types.

Paddington is a most optimistic bear — always certain of himself and his abilities, never letting any situation get the better of him, and always looking on the bright side of things. Being accident-prone never dulls his spirit — this is largely due to his being born with paws rather than hands, and that obviously is not his fault. While Paddington is an avid shopper, he could never be called materialistic, since all of his possessions can fit into his small suitcase. He could drive a hard bargain, and he once won a jackpot of £500 on a quiz show and very generously donated the majority of it to the Home for Retired Bears in Lima. Paddington is the personification of middle class values such as honesty, courtesy, respectfulness, and determination. He uses good manners, tips his hat to the ladies, and never complains.

Concerning Paddington's place within the Brown family, he is somewhat an enigma. He is at once a child, an adult, a worrisome poet, a loyal family member, a kind friend, and a lovable klutz. He sets about life with the innocence of a child and the stability of an adult, but with the sticky and accident-prone paws of a small bear. It is quite amusing to ponder that before Paddington, Michael Bond submitted several children's book ideas to publishers that were returned and rejected time and again, explaining, "we don't do fantasy." But the idea of a talking bear making his way halfway across the world to live in Notting Hill with a human family was welcomed with open arms!

Some have suggested that the reason that Paddington Bear was so wildly successful as compared to the other animal characters that Bond created is that those characters "retain too many of the natural characteristics of the animals on which the stories were based."[14] It is true that Paddington's character does not closely resemble the attributes of a real bear, Peruvian or otherwise. In fact, one of the most endearing of his qualities, and one that delights both children and adults alike, is his habit of mis-hearing, mis-understanding, and mis-construing the words, objects, and concepts that he encounters. For instance, in *Paddington Goes to Town,* Paddington gets confused about the word "ring," as in a wedding ring, versus its meaning to make a phone call (i.e. give Mrs. Brown a ring). This confusion leads to the wedding ring going missing at a wedding where Paddington was an usher, later to turn up on Paddington's paw, of all places. In the same book, Paddington mixes up "tee" and "tea" in his golf game, and mishears the word "stance" which he processes as "stamps," leading to further chaos. And really, what child or adult cannot relate to such an experience?

---

[14] Hunt, p. 34.

Through the years, the Paddington images were drawn by several talented artists, beginning with the first and perhaps most important, Peggy Fortnum. Born in 1919, Peggy Fortnum studied at the Central School of Arts and Crafts in London. Best known for her line illustrations, she began drawing book illustrations in 1944, for *Dorcas the Wooden Doll*. She later drew for such authors as Oscar Wilde, Kenneth Grahame, and Noel Streatfeild. She was already doing some work for Collins in London when she was commissioned to do the Paddington Bear artwork. The design was left pretty much up to her, and she quickly established his trademark "look." He wore a trilby hat at first, similar to one her father had worn. This later evolved into the characteristic ragtag bush hat. She required approximately six weeks to illustrate one book.

Marcus Crouch, well known for his reviews of children's books, once commented on the Paddington drawings, "The books owe as much to Peggy Fortnum for her drawings as Milne's do to E. H. Shepard; she not only captured the bear's appearance, his shagginess, and his deplorable hat, but his movements in a number of fluent action-pictures."[15] Fortnum found this comparison very flattering. Her work seems to suggest that the more she drew, the more she loved Paddington Bear, and she was able to capture all of his various moods in her sketches. Although her original illustrations were done in black and white, some were later colored by other artists, including her own niece, Caroline Nuttal-Smith. All of Paddington's subsequent illustrators—R. W. Alley, Fred Banbery, Ivor Wood, Barry Macey, David McKee, and John Lobban—stayed true to and consistent with her original drawings.

---

[15] Ash, p. 35.

R. W. Alley grew up an only child in Virginia, New York, Texas, South Carolina, and Maryland, and now resides in Rhode Island where he does his drawing from a studio in his home. He claims to have started drawing when he was two years old, and spent his childhood creating things from clay, cardboard, and whatever else was handy. He also made up stories and characters. He received an art history degree from Haverford College and toyed with the idea of becoming a lawyer. But not for long. After working as an artist for several greeting card companies, he began working as a freelance artist in 1985. He started illustrating for the Paddington books in 1997. Alley drew Paddington in the two most recent novels, *Paddington Here and Now* and *Paddington Races Ahead.* He also illustrated ten picture books, ten of the smaller format storybooks, and eight other books, including a cookbook and some of the compilations.

Fred Banbery was the illustrator for six of the Paddington picture books. Ivor Wood, besides being the designer for the original puppet in the first television series, also drew Paddington. His drawings were used in Paddington cartoon strips that were published in the *London Evening News* in the 1970s. David McKee, an illustrator and author in his own right, illustrated some of the second series of the smaller format Paddington picture books. He was already well known for his own books featuring King Rollo, Elmer the Elephant, and Mr. Benn. Barry Macey worked for Paddington & Co. as an in-house artist for several years, doing some of the drawing for older products and prints. He also illustrated *Paddington on Screen*, a compilation of the *Blue Peter* stories. John Lobban drew Paddington also for several books that were published in the 1990s.

With the development of Paddington's character in the stories and his growing popularity in England and beyond, it was only a matter of time until he would begin the journey from concept to physicality. In true Paddington fashion, his arrival as a tangible being was quite haphazard and somewhat unwitting. How did this journey come about?

Enter Shirley Clarkson. Clarkson was a lady who lived in England with her husband Eddie and two young children. Shirley struggled, you might say, to "find" herself throughout her growing up years. She was thoroughly educated, though she found very little to interest her in the area of academics. When she at last finished her schooling, it was with an art degree that she left behind the hallowed halls of academia. After several attempts at various jobs, she found a modicum of success designing and creating decorative items for the home, such as tea cozies, aprons, draught excluders, and the like. All of her designs were created by hand from her home, and sold to boutiques across England by her husband and sales representative, Eddie. And so she founded her business, called Gabrielle Designs, in the late 1960's. Sales were good, and outside help was hired to meet demand.

The Clarkson family was well acquainted with Paddington Bear, having read the books to their children over the years. In Shirley Clarkson's own words, the books "contained everything a child wants in a book: a bear, marmalade, sticky buns, ice cream, glue, soap suds, together with a character that epitomized what every adult admires: innocence, vulnerability, kindness, humour, politeness, and an unshakeable love and loyalty towards his friends."[16] An annual Christmas tradition was for Shirley to sew a stuffed animal for each of her two children to place above their stockings on Christmas morning. For this particular year, she determined to create a stuffed Paddington Bear to embody the charming character from the books. Shirley found herself extremely busy however, keeping up with the business demands while shuttling two children to school and to their various extracurricular activities, and Christmas was quickly approaching. In somewhat of a panic, she asked one of her assistants to begin work on the project, giving her only the sketches found in the books and her own ideas for the small creature to work from.

---

[16] Clarkson, **pp.** 71-72.

Upon arriving home after a very busy day, Shirley checked the workroom for any progress on the bear. To her surprise, she found the bear finished, complete with a coat, a posy of flowers in hand, and the tiniest pair of spectacles sitting on his nose. She was taken aback at the sight of him, later saying, "I recognized something in Paddington that was special, and knew immediately that this design wasn't just going to sit atop Jeremy and Joanna's Christmas stocking; it was going to become a Gabrielle product."[17] The Clarksons set about almost immediately making and selling more of the bears. Sure, copyright laws were considered, but Shirley and Eddie very naively assumed that if they gave the bear a different name, all would be well. The bear was quickly named "The Earl of Burghwallis" and off he went to market. Orders came rolling in. Even though the name was changed to protect the innocent, as it were, alas the merchants and happy customers immediately recognized him as Paddington of Darkest Peru, no less. Eddie, getting a little worried at this point, cautioned his merchants not to use the name "Paddington" in association with the lovable bear. The warnings fell on deaf ears, however, and Eddie arrived at one London shop to find a giant banner claiming, "Paddington Bear Comes to Town."

---

[17] Clarkson, p. 73.

Not surprisingly, the next morning the Clarksons were served legal papers, something to the effect that they should cease and desist or else pay substantial damages. A meeting was then arranged between Eddie and Michael Bond in the office of Bond's solicitor, Mr. Edlmann. The "Earl," a/k/a Paddington was also invited to attend, and he did. Bond immediately set Eddie at ease by assuring him that he had no intention of putting a stop to production of the bears. In fact, he stated that "it was the finest bear he had ever seen." The only issue then was the question of royalties, and the wise solicitor made quick work of drawing up an agreement which was amenable to both sides. Drawn up in 1972, Gabrielle Designs would have the exclusive right to sell the bears all over the world, with legal protection against any who thought to pirate the design.

Bond had "discovered" the bear when an acquaintance and owner of a small boutique near his home called to congratulate him on the product. Since Bond was unaware of its existence, he sent his assistant to the store to look into the matter. Bond had been quite taken with the likeness, later writing in his autobiography of his first vision, "it remains a classic of its kind — one which still gives me pleasure whenever I see it — and it served as a kind of yardstick when judging other products….It was created with love and it was born with that indefinable something known as star quality. You either have it or you don't."[18] Ultimately, Bond ended up in the Clarkson home over a gourmet meal cooked by Eddie, and remarking, "what a delightful setting it was in which to have his beloved bears created."[19]

---

[18] Clarkson, p. 73.

[19] Clarkson, p. 80.

And create they did. By August of 1973, 1,800 bears had been sold, a staggering number to the Clarksons, who never imagined the sharp upward direction the sales would take. No advertising was needed. Trade fairs, not necessary. Clarkson asserts the reason for the seemingly effortless success: "It was the character of Paddington himself—that helpless appeal of the little bear lost, who was just begging to be picked up and loved."[20]

---

[20] Clarkson, p. 83.

Keeping the toy bear true to his "roots" and consistent with the books proved challenging at times. At one point, it was decided that the bear looked much better when standing, and this was easily accomplished by putting the bear in some Wellington boots, a child's size 4 to be exact. The only problem was, Paddington did not wear boots in any of the books' illustrations. The solution: Bond added a story in the next book in which Paddington would acquire a new pair of boots. As it happened, Paddington had an adventure in a department store with some pajamas that wouldn't sell, simply because they were hideous. However, when Paddington himself modeled the same pajamas in a store window, they began flying off the shelf! The store manager was so impressed that, as a reward, Paddington could pick anything in the store for himself. And as fate would have it, he settled on a pair of shiny red boots.

One might think that was the end of that. However, soon children all over the world were finding that Paddington had no feet! To aid in more efficient production, Gabrielle had opted to omit the feet in favor of "stubs," since they would be covered by the boots anyway. Young fans were shocked to discover this when the bear's boots were removed, and letters poured in. Likewise, apologies poured out, and along with them a promise to alter the process in order to give Paddington feet. Once again, an expensive lesson to learn, but learned nonetheless.

The very last step of the production process may be little known and rather shocking. After Paddington had been sewn, stuffed, and dressed, a firm karate chop was delivered squarely to his cute little nose! But no worries — Paddington is not hurt by this, being a very resilient bear. Quite the contrary, this action is believed to be the "secret of his expression — part cheeky, part hard stare, part an indefinable Paddington-ness."[21] It is not until this step is completed that Paddington may be packed and shipped.

---

[21] Ash, p. 64.

As Paddington sales took off, Gabrielle Designs was forced to discontinue production of its other designs to keep up with bear production. The Paddington books were then being translated into twenty-six languages, and bears were being shipped worldwide, including Japan, France, Germany, Australia, New Zealand, Bermuda, and Scandinavia. Marketing the bears in America was slightly more complicated, and in 1973, the Clarksons relinquished all overseas rights to Eden Toys Inc. in New York. This was at the same time both exciting and vexing to Shirley Clarkson. On one hand, it was great to be expanding to such a broad market, but the downside was that the bears would now be mass-produced. The toy company opted to create their own patterns rather than use the original Clarkson design. Shirley felt that the U.S.-made bears never had quite the same expression, reasoning that "we had always thought of Paddington as a living, loving, breathing bear; whereas Eden referred to him as having a merchantable rate."[22]

---

[22] Clarkson, p. 115.

Unfortunately, counterfeit products also made an appearance on the market. Eddie chased the pirates with a vengeance, with mixed results. One retailer refused to back down and was taken to the High Court in London. This particular retailer produced a stuffed bear wearing a duffle coat, wellies, and a felt hat, but with a red, white, and blue ribbon around the hat, and called him "Wellington." The case was settled out of court, but a precedent was set that would protect the Clarksons and Paddington from future infractions. The court established that if a stuffed bear wore two of the three main Paddington Bear pieces, those being the coat, boots, and hat, it was considered counterfeit and therefore a copyright infringement.

The best year for sales was 1978, with just under 87,000 bears sold. As the brand increased in popularity, other products began to emerge: stationery, bedding, and ceramic figures. Retail shops now opened in London and later in Bath. Clarkson herself began to seek other marketing ventures, first designing a mini Paddington, a small bean bag which she called Beanie. He had shorter fur, no boots, was fat and cuddly, and with Bond's approval the toy was marketed. Michael had only one criticism—the original design had the toy stuffed with split peas, and out of his concern for world hunger, he requested that a non-edible stuffing be found. Clarkson instead stuffed the bear with polystyrene beads, and sales topped 100,000.

Problems began for Clarkson and Gabrielle Designs soon after, when Eddie became very ill and bedridden. It was terrible timing — it was the peak of Paddington sales; they had hired a useless office manager who quickly ran off a long-time worker; their daughter Joanna was also seriously ill; their mischievous son Jeremy was expelled from school; and a safety issue was discovered with their stuffing machine. Despite the hardships, Shirley chose this time to launch yet another product — the Paddington Bear suitcase, containing a toy marmalade sandwich, a picture of Aunt Lucy, and a Peruvian coin. For a variety of reasons, this project ended in disaster. The tiny cases were found to be defective and returns were coming in faster than orders were going out.

Soon after, in February 1979, some bears began to turn up with defective eyes. Some eyes were becoming glazed, and others were simply falling out. It was discovered that the eye supplier was using a cheaper plastic material, and also that the hole in the accompanying metal washers was slightly larger than previous products. True to Paddington's adventurous optimism, each returned bear underwent a quite serious operation. An incision had to be made in the back of Paddington's head, he was partially unstuffed, the eyes replaced, then re-stuffed and sewn up. Perhaps the most difficult part of the operation was returning each bear to its rightful owner. Since all Paddingtons created by Gabrielle were handmade and therefore one of a kind, it was imperative that each mended bear be returned to the same address from which it was sent. Each "recovering" bear was placed in a box marked with a red cross and accompanied by a marmalade sandwich (of course) and a letter explaining that Paddington (now sporting a bandage on his head) had been quite a good patient. The cost of the fiasco was estimated at £40,000.

Also in 1979, Shirley's father died unexpectedly. They had been very close and he had been heavily involved with the business. It was a great loss to Clarkson, but she forged ahead with another product. The character of Aunt Lucy would now be embodied in a design which included "aging" grey fur, full Peruvian dress, and black bowler hat. Though predictably sales did not match those of her nephew, Aunt Lucy did okay.

Gabrielle Designs would produce several other "characters" through the years, but none so popular as the beloved Paddington. In 1995, shortly after Eddie's death, Shirley sold the company and retired, declaring herself "heartily sick and tired of stuffing."[23] The company did not fare so well under the new owners, and declared bankruptcy in 1998. Shirley Clarkson sums the story of her career by recalling a chance conversation with a lady on a train. When asked what she did for a living, Shirley replied, "I make Paddington Bears." The stranger responded, "You must have brought so much pleasure to so many people." Clarkson would certainly like to think so.

---

[23] Clarkson, p. 196.

After the success of *A Bear Called Paddington*, Collins commissioned a second book, and *More About Paddington* was published in 1959. Bond wrote one book per year until 1962, and then two per year until 1970. After that, the books were less frequent as he worked on other writings. In 1963, *Paddington at Large* made the *New York Times* "100 Outstanding Books of the Year for Young Readers." In 1969, Brenda Bond compiled a book of quotes taken from the first eight books, one for each day of the year, and it was marketed as *Paddington's Birthday Book*. Brenda reportedly kept a copy for visitors to sign on their birthday page, and always found it interesting to match up each person with her or his "birthday quote."

In 1970, *Paddington Takes the Air* was published, and with this book Paddington began his very own writing career, writing letters to booksellers to help promote the books (with a little help from Michael) and signing with his paw print. In 1972, some of the prior Paddington stories were condensed and simplified for preschoolers and introduced as the "Young Set." Some critics have indicated that these picture books for early readers do not serve Paddington or Bond well, and advise that kids simply wait until they are old enough to read the full original novels to get the full flavor of Paddington's personality and character (to which Paddington would likely respond with one of his signature hard stares).[24] In 1983, *Paddington's Story Book* was published, which was a compilation of the most favorite stories over the years, featuring the colored artwork of Peggy Fortnum.

---

[24] Hunt, p.34.

What might be characterized as the main body of work in the Paddington series consists of thirteen novels, beginning with the very first book, *A Bear Called Paddington* published in 1958, to the most recent, *Paddington Races Ahead* published in 2012. The fourteenth novel is currently in process and is set to be published in late 2014. The novels are full length chapter books, with each chapter a stand-alone story in most of them. The novels, in order of publication are:

A Bear Called Paddington (1958). In Paddington's debut, Mr. and Mrs. Brown have a most peculiar experience at the railway station, after arriving there to greet their daughter Judy who was returning home from school, when they come upon a little lost bear. The poor thing was found sitting atop his battered suitcase with nothing else but a small sign attached to his neck with the simple plea, "Please look after this bear. Thank you." Unable to resist his charm, the Browns agree to offer him a place to stay and officially bestow the name of Paddington upon him, after the station. The Browns' family, including children Judy and Jonathan and housekeeper Mrs. Bird, quickly accepted Paddington into their hearts, and life would never be the same! In January 1960, this book was translated into Swedish, Danish, and Dutch. In 1967, the Japanese version was first published.

More About Paddington (1959). In the second book of the series, Paddington's adopted family learns that, well, you just never know what sort of chaos their new charge will find himself in. And the lovable bear doesn't deny it, admitting that, "Things happen to me—I'm that sort of bear." In this book, he will try his hand at interior decorating, photography, and a little detective work, resulting in the inevitable adventures. In 1965 the first two books were combined into a single volume marketed as *The Adventures of Paddington*.

Paddington Helps Out (1960). Somehow trouble always seems to find the irresistible Paddington. "Oh dear!" said Paddington, "I'm in trouble again." Ever striving to be a helpful bear, in this book Paddington catches a fish in his hat, attends an auction with his friend Mr. Gruber, attempts a carpentry project for Mr. Curry, and tries his paw at making dumplings for the sickly Mr. and Mrs. Brown. It seems that none of his projects turn out as planned, however, but not to worry, Paddington will be sure to save the day!

Paddington Abroad (1961). On a family trip to France, Paddington gets himself into one scrape after another. It seems Paddington is put in charge of the "eyetinnery," much to the dismay of Mrs. Bird ("There's no knowing where we might end up.") Paddington goes on to be the only bear ever to ride in the acclaimed Tour de France, and "accidentally" wins! Other hijinks include Paddington becoming a substitute drummer for a local band, an unpleasant episode with a fortune teller, and a boating trip which finds the family marooned on a deserted island — temporarily, of course.

Paddington at Large (1962). "Even Paddington can't come to much harm in half an hour," or so Mrs. Brown thought. But leave it to Paddington, who manages to hang Mr. Curry's lawnmower in a tree, create quite a disaster in a toffee-making attempt, and set fire to Father Christmas' beard! While attending a concert outing in which Schubert's *Unfinished Symphony* is to be performed, Paddington becomes quite disturbed that the orchestra would be so inconsiderate as to play a song that is not even finished, and sets out to complain to "Mr. Sherbert" himself. Instead, he unwittingly finds himself a part of the show!

Paddington Marches On (1964). In this novel, the endearing bear is found at an orange marmalade tasting party. Says Mrs. Bird, "I've never known such a bear for smelling things out." Feeling most enthusiastic at his good fortune, he nevertheless ends up in a barrel of marmalade and manages to set off an avalanche in the warehouse. Paddington also finds the inevitable adventures when he "helps" Mr. Curry with his plumbing problem, visits a wax museum and ends up in the "Chamber of Horrors," and joins a cricket match at Jonathan's school. He also finds himself the guest of honor at his own surprise party, where he learns that he will be returning to Peru to share in Aunt Lucy's 100th birthday celebration!

Paddington at Work (1966). After returning from Peru, Paddington wastes no time finding new adventures. He unknowingly invests in the stock market at the hand of a crooked con artist, but turns the tables by having him arrested. When he spends a day as an assistant barber, he tries out the electric clippers on an unsuspecting customer, resulting in an unsightly bald spot. After an unsuccessful attempt to make things right with a little glue and some hair clippings, Mr. Gruber once again comes to his rescue. In the final chapter, Paddington performs ballet at Judy's dance recital!

Paddington Goes to Town (1968). "Things" just continue happening to the Peruvian bear in this novel, when he joins Mr. Curry's golf outing as his caddie. This adventure unfortunately ends in Mr. Curry being hospitalized and Paddington playing a sneaky role in his eventual recovery. Paddington also finds himself as the chief cook for a fancy dinner party, where he serves his "baked elastic," creating quite a memorable experience for the guests. Another adventure has Paddington as an usher at a wedding, where the wedding ring turns up missing and the fire department must get involved!

Paddington Takes the Air (1970).
Paddington takes an interest in sewing, sleuthing, and ballroom dancing in the ninth novel. A hilarious adventure ensues when he tries out his "new" sewing machine to make alterations to Mr. Curry's trousers. The final chapter has Paddington at his first ball, and dancing with none other than the hostess herself, Mrs. Smith-Cholmley. Things predictably do not end well, however, when it is determined that his claws have stuck in the straps of her shoes and, if that wasn't enough, somehow a marmalade sandwich makes its way down the back of her dress!

Paddington on Top (1974). The powers-that-be have determined that Paddington must attend school and he excitedly agrees. However, after a day of misadventures, misunderstandings, and general havoc-wreaking, the idea is soon abandoned. On a trip to the beach for Paddington's birthday, he unintentionally invents the sport of "parachute-skiing" after enrolling in Signor Alberto's Ski School. Finally, Paddington attends a rugby match with a Peruvian team, where, much to his surprise, one of the visiting fans is his Aunt Lucy. Trouble follows, however, when Paddington helps Aunt Lucy select the perfect Christmas present for Mr. Brown!

Paddington Takes the Test (1979). In an amusing turn of events which could only involve a bear from Peru, Paddington attempts to take a driving test for Mr. Brown. His short stature and inability to see through the windshield unfortunately lead to his hitting the examiner's car. One chapter of the book finds Mr. Curry locked in a sauna. Guess who is behind it? The book culminates in the bear inadvertently volunteering to be sawn in half as part of a magic act!

Paddington Here and Now (2008). The twelfth novel, published on the 50th anniversary of *A Bear Called Paddington,* opens with Paddington's shopping cart being towed away and his being arrested. The hysterical antics continue with a Halloween party in which Mr. Curry tries Paddington's recipe for stir-fly soup, and Paddington's experience with a survey-taker that lands him front and center in a news report about illegal immigrants and "black market" organ transplants!

Paddington Races Ahead (2012). Paddington's life takes a decidedly "Olympic" turn, as he is confused for a Peruvian hurdler at the 2012 Olympic Games in London. Among other escapades, he tries to ride a bus using real oysters, instead of an "Oyster Card," which is a type of electronic ticket for London's mass transit system. In the spirit of the Games, Paddington employs the services of a personal trainer, only to find that exercise is not for him, since his short legs make exercising extremely difficult—but above all, becoming fit may mean giving up his sticky buns!

Love from Paddington (2014) is, in a sense, Paddington's autobiography. The book is a compilation of Paddington's letters over the years to his Aunt Lucy. It seems that Paddington is quite adept at letter writing, and in this book, readers will gain distinctive insight into his journey from Darkest Peru, his integration into the Brown family and British life, and his unique view of the world around him.

On several occasions, the stories from various books were combined and published under a single title. This was the case with *Paddington's Blue Peter Story Book,* which compiled the first seven stories written for the *Blue Peter Annual.* The book was published in 1973, and since Blue Peter was a British program and not familiar to Americans, it was marketed in the U.S. as *Paddington Takes to TV*. A similar compilation was done in 1982, titled *The Second Blue Peter Story Book* in Britain, and *Paddington on Screen* in the U.S. *Paddington's Story Book,* an anthology of several previous stories, was published in 1983. Another anthology comprised of five previous books was titled *A Bear Called Paddington* and was published in 1985.

In 1972, Bond began a new series of Paddington books aimed at younger children. These are generally referred to as the "picture books," and in many cases include shorter, simpler versions of the stories from the novels. In most of these books, each page has a full color illustration. The picture books consist of the following:

> *Paddington Bear (1972).* This first picture book of the "young set" series gives preschoolers an introduction to the very special "rare sort of bear" from Darkest Peru.
>
> *Paddington Bear in the Garden (1972).* Paddington loves the Browns' garden, and sets out to make it more interesting, with his characteristic sense of adventure.
>
> *Paddington at the Circus (1973).* The circus is in town, and Paddington has a front row seat. He is astounded by the sights there, but wait…there's a man hanging by a rope high above Paddington's head! What else is there to do but lend a paw to help the man?

Paddington Goes Shopping (UK-1973)/ Paddington's Lucky Day (US-1974). Paddington visits a brand new supermarket, worries with a shopping cart, and his day turns out quite grandly when he wins a prize!

Paddington at the Seaside (1975). A visit to the beach includes a "Punch and Judy" show, but Paddington is not impressed and must interrupt! Hilarity ensues.

Paddington at the Tower (1975). Paddington's visit to the famous Tower of London ends up getting him into some trouble involving his suitcase full of (what else?) marmalade sandwiches.

These first six titles in the picture book series were also published in paperback by Pan Piccolo, and the same titles were later combined in an anthology titled *Paddington's Picture Book* in 1986. Other picture books were compiled using abridged stories based on the television series, published as "Collins Cubs Books" from 1977 through 1980, including:

Paddington at the Station

Paddington Takes a Bath

Paddington's New Room

Paddington in the Kitchen

Paddington Does it Himself

Paddington Goes to the Sales

Paddington Hits Out

Paddington's Birthday Party

Paddington on the River

Paddington Weighs In

Paddington in Touch

Paddington and Aunt Lucy

The second series of picture books include the following:

> *Paddington and the Knickerbocker Rainbow (UK-1984)*, also marketed as *Paddington and the Tutti Frutti Rainbow (US-1998)*. Will the bad weather ruin the Browns' beach outing? Not really — and with Paddington along, it is sure to be an adventure, as he finds himself in a close encounter with a rather large ice cream sundae.

Paddington at the Zoo (1984). Paddington packs six marmalade sandwiches for his trip to the zoo...and doesn't get to eat a single one! Find out why in this beautiful picture book.

Paddington at the Fair (1985). Paddington finds high adventure when he has an outing to Hampstead Fair with the Browns, where he tries out several amusement rides.

Paddington's Painting Exhibition (UK-1985); Paddington's Art Exhibition (US-1986). Paddington attends an art exhibition with Mr. Gruber, then decides to have his own exhibition. He soon finds that painting is not as easy as it seems, especially when you have paws!

Paddington at the Palace (1986). Paddington takes a trip to Buckingham Palace with his friend Mr. Gruber. But the crowd is so large, he can't see the changing of the guards! Whatever will he do to solve his problem? A very unexpected person comes to his rescue!

Paddington Minds the House (1986). In what turns out to be yet another very sticky adventure, Paddington does some "cleaning" and bakes a cake to surprise the Browns.

Paddington and the Marmalade Maze (1987). Mr. Gruber joins Paddington for yet another outing, this time to Hampton Court, where Paddington succeeds in attracting a crowd of tourists eager to follow him home. But never fear, he finds a way to lose them in the Marmalade Maze!

Paddington's Busy Day (1987). What "dark" adventures will Paddington find when he determines to tidy up the loft at Number Thirty-two Windsor Gardens?

Paddington's Magical Christmas (1988). Paddington tries to understand some of the mystery surrounding Christmas in England. In any event, the holiday is quite merry and there is a big parade to boot!

Paddington on the River (1989). Paddington finds adventure on the river with his favorite family in this sliding picture book.

Paddington's Disappearing Trick (1992). Paddington is at it again. When he attempts some magic tricks at his birthday party, things do not go exactly as planned.

Paddington Bear and the Christmas Surprise (1997). Paddington has been saving his money and is ready to take the Browns on a Christmas shopping trip to Barkridge's. The inevitable chaos ensues, but Santa Claus assists Paddington in saving the day.

Paddington Bear and the Busy Bee Carnival (1998), also marketed as *Paddington at the Carnival (2010)*. Paddington and Mr. Gruber embark on an adventure at the carnival, searching for things beginning with the letter "B."

Paddington's Party Tricks (2000). Paddington throws Mr. Gruber a birthday party where he puts on a magic show that ends up with the bothersome Mr. Curry getting an unexpected soaking!

Paddington Goes to the Hospital (2001). Paddington lands in a hospital after attempting to remove his kite from a tree using "rather unorthodox methods." Join him on this new adventure as he learns all about things that go on inside a hospital.

Paddington at the Beach, also marketed as *Paddington, King of the Castle (2009).* Paddington visits the beach, builds a sand castle, and has a counting adventure with the seagulls.

Paddington at the Rainbow's End (2009). Paddington spends the day shopping and decides that there is one color in the rainbow that he especially likes.

Paddington Goes for Gold (2012). Paddington attends a family sports competition with his adopted family and learns that winning isn't everything. Not surprisingly, a sticky situation arises.

Some later picture books and board books were collaborations with Bond's daughter, Karen Bond Jankel. Paddington board books and pop-up books for the very young reader include:

Paddington's Pop-up Book (1977)

Paddington at Home (1980)

Paddington's Shopping Adventure (1981)

Paddington Learns a Lesson (1981)

Paddington's Birthday Treat (1981)

Paddington and the Snowbear (1981)

Paddington at the Launderette (1981)

Paddington at the Airport (1986, with Karen Bond Jankel*)*

Paddington Posts a Letter (1986, with Karen Bond Jankel*)*

Paddington's London (1986, with Karen Bond Jankel*)*

Paddington Goes Out (1989)

Paddington Works Hard (1989)

Paddington Has Fun (1989)

Paddington at the Seashore (1992)

Paddington Up and About (1999)

Paddington Goes to Market (1999)

Paddington Dresses Up (2004)

Paddington Buggy Book (2011)

Paddington All Day (2014)

Other publications, including activity, learning, and just-for-fun books, include:

Paddington's Birthday Book (1969, with Brenda Bond*)*

Paddington Goes to the States (1976)

The Great Big Paddington Book (1976)

Paddington's Loose-End Book: An ABC of Things to Do (1976)

Paddington's Party Book (1976)

Paddington's Shopping Trip (1976)

Paddington Bear Songbook (1976, with Alfred Bradley*)*

Fun and Games with Paddington (1977)

Paddington on Stage: Plays for Children (1977, with Alfred Bradley*)*

Paddington's Cartoon Book (1979)

Paddington's Day of Action (1983)

Paddington's Clock Book (1986, with Karen Bond Jankel*)*

Paddington's Bus Ride (1986, with Karen Bond Jankel*)*

Paddington's Wheel Book (1986, with Karen Bond Jankel*)*

Paddington's Numbers (1987, with Karen Bond Jankel*)*

Paddington's Colours (1987, with Karen Bond Jankel*)*

Paddington's 1st Puzzle Book (1987, with Karen Bond Jankel*)*

Paddington's 2nd Puzzle Book (1987, with Karen Bond Jankel*)*

The Paddington Activity Book (1989)

The Giant Paddington Story Book (1989)

Paddington's ABC (1990)

Paddington's Opposites (1990)

Paddington's 1 2 3 (1991)

Paddington's Busy Week (1991)

Paddington Meets the Queen (1991)

Paddington's Disappearing Trick (1992)

Paddington Does the Decorating (1993)

Paddington's Picnic (1993)

Paddington Rides On (1993)

Paddington's Things I Do (1994)

Paddington's Things I Feel (1994)

Paddington Makes a Mess (1994)

Paddington's First Word Book (1998)

Paddington Bear: My Scrapbook (1999)

Paddington Bumper Colouring and Sticker Fun (2000)

Paddington Bear Travel Fun for Busy Bears (2006)

Paddington Puzzle and Play Book (2008)

Paddington: My Book of Marmalade (2008)

Paddington: The Arrival (2009), with jigsaw puzzle

Paddington and the Disappearing Sandwich (2009)

Paddington's Guide to London (2011)

Paddington's Cookery Book (2011)

With so many titles in publication, it is indeed hard to imagine what Paddington could possibly come up with next, as it seems that every possible situation has already been conceived. That Bond continues to create storylines and keep the stories alive and fresh is truly a tribute to his imagination and his skill.

After first appearing in books and print, Paddington Bear made his debut on radio in 1965, with *Paddington Helps Out* on the BBC program *Children's Hour*. Soon thereafter, another BBC program, *Story Time*, also aired *Paddington Helps Out*, as well as *More about Paddington*. In 1966, the Delyse Record Company released four of the Paddington stories in a total of seven records in the U.K.

In 1984, Paddington released his own gold record—it was literally recorded on translucent gold vinyl and featured songs from *Paddington Bear's Magical Musical*. On the record, released by Audiotrax, Paddington belts out tunes with titles such as: "Down in Darkest Peru," "Marmalade 'n' Me," "Wellington Waltz," and "Never Go Out Without a Label."

A new audio collection of books on CD is set to be released in August 2014. The boxed set includes four books: *A Bear Called Paddington*, *More About Paddington*, *Paddington Here and Now*, and *Paddington Races Ahead*, as read by Stephen Fry and Jim Broadbent.

The first attempt at putting Paddington Bear on the silver screen was time-consuming and unproductive. Bond worked with Alec Snowden, whom he describes as a producer of the "old school" tradition. He had "never adjusted to the fact that television was here to stay, as inevitable as the wheel, whether people liked it or not," according to Michael.[25] Production of the pilot started badly when British Rail wouldn't allow the use of Paddington Station, forcing them to use the more obscure and somewhat forlorn Marylebone Station on a Sunday morning, not exactly the hustle and bustle described in the book.

---

[25] Bond, p. 182.

Snowden also insisted that Paddington Bear be played by a midget in bearskin. The costume actually looked pretty good in person, but on camera every fault was magnified. The visible seams in the costume were reminiscent of Frankenstein. The facial features were fixed on the papier mâché head, so that facial expressions were portrayed by the midget falling down with his feet in the air to register surprise and running in circles to express excitement, all in all a quite unpleasant spectacle. The actor could lift his hat, but could not feel exactly where to set it back down again. Because of these challenges, the character scarcely even resembled Paddington—in Bond's words, "Anything less like the bear of my dreams would be hard to imagine…Nobody in their right mind would have taken him home to live with them."[26]

---

[26] Bond, p. 183.

As if things weren't bad enough, the actor had difficulty hearing inside the head, so that from the time that "Action!" was called, filming was already off to a bad start. It was painfully obvious that Paddington was not speaking the lines, so the idea was borne to create a separate electronic head. By the use of hand-operated gimbals, some expressions could be exhibited — rolling and blinking eyes, shaking and nodding of the head, and moving of the mouth in an attempt to lip-synch the dialogue. This method too met with problems — the eyes would certainly blink, but not necessarily in unison. Michael noted later that "the art of making television characters that are a sophisticated mixture of electronics and live animators had a long way to go before the arrival on the scene of Jim Henson and his Muppets set new standards."[27] Nevertheless, scripts were written and financial backing was sought. A pilot was finally completed, but Bond was not pleased with it and the project was abandoned until a better method could be found.

---

[27] Bond, p. 185.

In 1965, Bond made an appearance on the BBC's television program *Blue Peter*, beginning a long-term relationship with the show and the *Blue Peter Storybooks*. The show had a magazine format, with one or more hosts and a wide range of segments consisting of arts and crafts projects, interviews, news items, viewer and presenter challenges, and the like. Since leaving the BBC to write full-time, Bond had been approached by them, seeking ideas for new children's programming. As it happened, Bond had been working on a series called *The Herbs*, starring Parsley the Lion. It was in the production of this series that Bond met two men who would later be instrumental in furthering Paddington's career in television, Graham Clutterbuck and Ivor Wood.

Clutterbuck was a commercial producer for FilmFair and ran the Paris office of the Los Angeles based company. Wood began his career painting backgrounds for animated advertisements. Along with Serge Danot, he created the *Magic Roundabout* series. Wood was particularly skilled at making a three-dimensional puppet from a two-dimensional character, manipulated to simulate movement in a technique known as "stop-frame photography." The technique was used in films such as the 1933 *King Kong*, but had not before been used in children's programming. The process at that time was very painstaking, and it could take weeks to produce one five-minute program.

Both Clutterbuck and Wood eventually returned to England, Clutterbuck to set up a FilmFair office in London, and Wood to work on the Wombles, a very popular children's show of the day. Around this time, Wood also started working on an idea he had for filming Paddington. After showing it to Bond over lunch one day, he liked it immediately and soon struck a deal with both Wood and Clutterbuck. Bond set about writing scripts, Clutterbuck worked on the production end, and Wood began creating the Paddington model. It would be only nine inches high, composed of steel rods and ball-bearing joints. He was highly detailed, so that even the fingers of his paws were movable and able to clasp the all-important marmalade sandwich and other, less significant, objects. Wood also designed the sets for the backgrounds. Since several would be needed to portray the different stories, it was decided that the scenes would be black and white and only two-dimensional, with the only three-dimensional model being Paddington himself.

A pilot was produced and accepted by the BBC. The team then set about addressing various concerns which had been encountered while producing the pilot. Bond decided that Paddington wouldn't actually speak, but instead the stories would be narrated. There were several actors interested in reading for the part, but in auditions they attempted to sound bear-like and it was all very awkward. The English actor Michael Hordern was approached about the part. Replying, "I don't do voices," he was almost immediately hired, and his was quickly deemed to be the perfect voice for Paddington. The use of a narrator eliminated the need for Paddington to have his own voice, and with it the need to animate or lip-sync his facial movements. Narration would also "allow one to be a party to Paddington's thoughts and idiosyncratic powers of reasoning…" Bond even found himself hearing Hordern's voice as he wrote and tailored the scripts with it in mind.[28]

---

[28] Bond, p. 190.

The BBC commissioned thirty programs based on the original stories from the books. It was a challenge to condense a Paddington story into a five-minute program, since most stories represented about twenty minutes' reading time, but condense they did. The scripts were written, equating to about one minute per page, with Paddington hopefully extricating himself from whatever trouble he was in by the end of page four. The episodes aired in 1975, and were sold around the world and translated into several languages.

Throughout the 1970's, Bond and Clutterbuck would routinely travel to France and the Marche International Programmes-Television, which is an annual television festival aimed at selling programs to the world market. Bond speaks fondly of the trips with his friend, with many tales of their experiences in the French countryside, the friends and acquaintances they made, and in true Paddington fashion, the scrapes they often found themselves in.

In 1979 a second series of twenty-six episodes aired and the show became the first British animated series to win a major American film award — a silver medal at the New York Film and Television Festival. In contrast to the earlier attempt by Snowden, Wood was able to preserve Paddington's "dignity and warmth."

The time- and labor-intensive programming had a budget of around £60,000 for the first thirty episodes. Since the BBC would cover only about one-fifth of that, the financial gap would need to be bridged with sales of related merchandise. The prior success of the Wombles series had set the stage for such a merchandising effort. Much of the success of Paddington-related sales could be attributed to the hard work and salesmanship of Eddie Clarkson, who tirelessly pursued only the most exclusive outlets for Paddington Bear products to be sold (or seen). While his strategy seemed counterintuitive to the mass marketing approach, the fact that Paddington appeared only in the most worthy boutiques may have contributed to the bear's *Je ne sais quoi,* and making him a symbol of reliability and integrity. By the early 1980's, Paddington began to appear in magazines, many times unnamed, but rarely unrecognized.

The merchandising and commercialization of Paddington was challenging at times to Bond. He would very often consult Paddington when faced with decisions about this product and that product. If he received a hard stare in response, the product idea would be quashed, as was the case of the Paddington toilet paper roll and the furry wastepaper can with removable Paddington head.

In the U.S., a television series was created by combining five five-minute episodes to make one thirty-minute program. It aired on the Public Broadcasting Service (PBS) in 1981 and was later also offered on the premium cable channel, Home Box Office (HBO). Selling the programs to the American market presented its own challenges, even more than the British market. The language had to be Americanized, changing words like "headmaster" to the American equivalent, "principal." Also, in the American market audience ratings ruled the day and therefore audiences were catered to. More color was added to Wood's previously black and white backgrounds and other seemingly insignificant changes were made. After three films, Bond tired of the restrictions and criticisms and no further episodes were filmed.

Both the British and American versions of the series were also released as videos. Wood then set out to create several half hour special programs, having perfected and improved the stop-frame animation of Paddington by adding such elements as water to the program. Bond once commented that "such was the state of Ivor's art Paddington could do anything he liked—he could even dance something like 'Singin' in the Rain,'" which he heartily did, and with Gene Kelly's full approval.[29]

In the early 1970's, Bond worked with Alfred Bradley, who was a BBC Radio drama producer, on a stage version of his stories. Paddington first appeared on stage in 1973 in a musical, *The Adventures of a Bear Called Paddington* at Nottingham Playhouse. In this version, Bond's wife Brenda wrote the song lyrics to the music of Herbert Chappell. One of the great challenges with putting Paddington Bear on stage is that of dialogue. In the stories, Paddington has little to say in the way of dialogue. According to Bond, "The humour lies mostly in the reader being a privileged party to the workings of his mind. Once you start giving Paddington too much dialogue you run the risk of making him seem either foolish or rude, both of which are totally out of character."[30]

In 1974, the same show was staged in London's Duke of York Theatre. In 1983, *Paddington Bear's Magical Musical* was produced by Bill Kenwright, from which an album was also released. A new version of *The Adventures of a Bear Called Paddington* appeared in 2003 and toured theatres all over the U.K. In 2005, the Polka Theatre staged *A Bear Called Paddington* at Wimbledon.

---

[29] Ash, p. 80.

[30] Bond, p. 187.

Presenting Paddington on stage was not without its challenges, not the least of which an actor was required to dress and perform in a bearskin, risking heatstroke. Whereas the stories and television shows were mostly narrated, a stage performance requires much more dialogue. Size is also an issue — were the character depicted as scaled in the books, he would be approximately three feet tall, but when an adult dons a bear suit and boots, he seems gigantic. Some workarounds were attempted; one actor sported a painted face with a black ping pong ball serving as his nose. The result of this was one sweltering actor chasing his nose across the stage when he developed a bad cold and runny nose.

Other stage disasters include a wayward British Rail trolley landing in the orchestra pit and a Paddington actor no-show in which Paddington was then portrayed by the actress normally playing Judy's character. The lines were mostly improvised and the play began with Jonathan's character running on stage announcing that Judy had missed the train and couldn't make it. The performance reportedly continued its downhill course from there. Incidentally, the latter was the production attended by Michael and Sue on their first date.

At the time of this writing, the first Paddington movie is in the works, set to be released in late 2014. By all accounts, Paddington is expected to hit the big screen in true Paddington fashion! The European company Studiocanal is behind the production. David Heyman, of *Harry Potter* fame, will produce the film, which will feature both live action and computer-generated images. Studiocanal chairman Olivier Courson comments, "Paddington is beloved across generations throughout the world. Heyman has had tremendous success adapting great British literary works for cinema."[31] Paul King is directing the film, which is referred to as a "modern take" on Bond's books. Can it be that technology has finally reached the point where little lost bears can finally be depicted and portrayed on the big screen with the dignity and respect that are rightfully deserved? One can only hope.

---

[31] "Paddington Bear Set for Big Screen Makeover." www.bbc.com/new/entertainment-arts.

From all indications, the film will be as classic and high quality as the books. Colin Firth, British star of film, television, and theater and Academy Award winner, was originally cast as the voice of Paddington. However, according to producer David Heyman, Firth sensed early on that his voice was not a good fit and there was mutual agreement to end the relationship. Instead, Ben Whishaw, the British star of both screen and stage, replaced Firth as the bear's voice, and was an immediate hit with the production team. Director Paul King commented that after Whishaw's audition, "[I] slowly found myself hearing his voice when I was thinking about Paddington. He breathes and he speaks and he sounds like Paddington." Ironically, Whishaw admits that he was not familiar with the Paddington Bear books as a child and for that reason auditioned with some trepidation, and that the whole recording process is baffling to him. "I just arrive and wear this funny helmet that has a camera attached to it. It's highly mysterious to me. I just see what they've done on screen, which is really beautiful and very exciting."[32]

---

[32] "Ben Whishaw Cast as New Paddington Bear." www.bbc.com/new/entertainment-arts.

The movie also will star Nicole Kidman as Millicent, a wicked museum taxidermist who is on Paddington's trail, and Hugh Bonneville as Mr. Brown. Other cast members include:

- Sally Hawkins as Mrs. Brown;
- Julie Walters as Mrs. Bird;
- Samuel Joslin as Jonathan Brown;
- Madeleine Harris as Judy Brown;
- Jim Broadbent as Mr. Gruber; and
- Peter Capaldi as Mr. Curry.

The film begins much as the original book, with Paddington arriving at Paddington Station. However, his background story is slightly different. In the film version, Aunt Lucy, because of a chance meeting with an English explorer who visited Peru, set her sights on sending Paddington to London. When her home is destroyed by an earthquake, she gets him on board a British-bound boat as a stowaway. Paddington vows to find the elusive explorer of his Aunt Lucy's story whilst he takes up "temporary" residence with the Browns. Millicent, the evil taxidermist, enters the picture, sets her sights on Paddington, and the bear must then find a way to escape her sinister plan.

Anyone with a stellar career that spans decades such as Paddington's is sure to amass certain awards and distinctions along the way, and he is no exception. Some of the honors listed below may seem very minor by human standards, but by Peruvian bear standards they are all, well, quite significant.

- In January 1959, *A Bear called Paddington* was honored as "The Best Children's Novel" of 1958 by the journal *Books and Bookmen.*
- In 1968, Lady Aitken owned a horse which was named Paddington Bear.
- A rock band called "The Paddington Bears" was formed in New Zealand in 1969.
- Paddington became the mascot and figurehead of the Make It Grow Club, the children's arm of Action Medical Research, a popular U.K. charity which seeks to improve the health of babies and children.
- Paddington was depicted in a four-foot-tall floral sculpture at Parade Gardens in Bath, as a part of the 1978 "Britain in Bloom" competition.

- Also in 1978, a 45-inch Paddington in a glass case was unveiled at Paddington Station.
- *Washington Post* fashion editor Nina S. Hyde lists Paddington Bear as a member of the "In Crowd" of 1980. He was accompanied on the list by, among others, Meryl Streep, Bruce Springsteen, and "cotton undies." Oh my.
- *Paddington Goes to the Movies* received an Emmy nomination for "Outstanding Children's Program" in 1981.
- Marking his 25th anniversary in 1983, Paddington was featured in a special Christmas display at Selfridge's, the British department store where Michael Bond purchased the very first "Paddington."
- In 1988, Hanna-Barbera was contracted to produce Paddington's stories in a cell animated program.
- Paddington scored his own 29-foot-tall balloon in the famous Macy's Thanksgiving Day Parade in 1990. But wait, he's set to appear again in 2014, the 88th annual parade, this time as a

whopping 60 foot tall and 34 foot wide high-flying balloon.
- When the Channel Tunnel, which links England to France beneath the English Channel, was first opened in 1994, Paddington Bear was chosen as the first to pass through. It was a grand adventure.
- In 1997, Cinar Films began the airing of thirteen Paddington episodes in England and Canada.
- Also in 1997, Michael Bond was awarded the OBE (Officer of the Order of the British Empire) for his contributions to children's literature.
- The London Toy and Model Museum honors Paddington's 40th anniversary with a special exhibit in 1998.
- In 2000, a life-sized bronze statue of Paddington was unveiled by Michael Bond on Paddington Station.
- Paddington went on a special tour of London to commemorate his 50th anniversary in 2008.
- In 2010, Paddington Bear became the "face" of Robertson's Marmalades, a popular brand in the U.K.

- A new version of *A Bear Called Paddington* became available for iPad, iPhone, and iTouch in 2011.
- Paddington was named as Britain's "Favourite Ever Animated Character" in 2012 at the British Animated Awards.
- In September 2013, filming of Paddington's new movie began.
- Paddington Bear appears on a U.K. postage stamp in the Royal Mail, one of several characters depicted to celebrate sixty years of children's television programs, released January 7, 2014.

In an effort to protect Paddington's image, Paddington and Company produced an amusing dossier in 1981, which both outlined the bear's salient features and certain features that are not in keeping with his image. From this, "we learn, for example, that while he is endowed with a strong sense of right and wrong, he is never mischievous, nor does he associate with other woodland creatures and, although things tend to happen to him, he seldom loses his dignity."[33]

---

[33] Ash, p. 92

Each year Bond receives thousands of letters from Paddington Bear fans across the world, some addressed only to Paddington Bear, London. It seems that if you happen to be a popular Peruvian bear in England, a postal code is not required. For many years, into the 1980's, each handwritten letter received a handwritten reply from Michael. In the late 1980's, however, Michael's wife began to help out by typing the response letters. One of Bond's favorite letters of all time simply reads, "Your stories make me have pictures in my head." This letter gave him a warm glow and "made it all worthwhile, for it rekindled the joy and excitement I felt when my father first introduced me to the *Magnet*."[34]

Through the years, the Paddington books have received critical acclaim from a variety of sources. There seems no doubt that Bond and Paddington have helped to fashion the landscape of children's literature for the 20th century and beyond. Following are some remarks by critics and other followers of the series.

- "Paddington has become part of the folklore of childhood…the humour of Paddington is largely visual; it is not what he is but what he does and how he does it

---

[34] Bond, p. 195.

that is funny." — Marcus Crouch, respected critic of children's literature and author of *The Nesbit Tradition: The Children's Novel in England, 1945-1970*
- "Paddington is a resolute little fellow of strong principles and few prejudices, full of resourcefulness and free of rancor: both the bear next door and something of a role model." — Pico Iyer, *Village Voice*
- "Most critics agree…that to think of Michael Bond is to think of Paddington." — Charles E. Matthews, *Dictionary of Literary Biography*
- "Well-meaning intentions go hilariously wrong, but beguiling innocence and dauntless enthusiasm always save the day." — Caroline Hunt, *Dictionary of Literary Biography*
- Ellen Lewis Buell, *New York Times Book Review*, cites Paddington's "endearing combination of bearishness and boyishness" for his popularity.
- "One is immensely impressed by the way each collection of stories comes up so fresh and full of humorous and highly original situations." — Eric Hudson, *Children's Book Review*

- "Although I write mainly children's books I don't write for children but more to please myself. If you write for children you run the risk of writing down. Although I believe very strongly that children's books are just as important as adult novels (and just as difficult!)." — Michael Bond

Michael Bond never set out to be a children's writer, and still seems surprised by it. In a 2012 interview at the release of the last Paddington novel *Paddington Races Ahead*, he was asked if he ever became sick of Paddington, to which he replied, "Yes. Whenever I finish a book I vow never to write another." Yet he always returns to the little bear, adding, "I can't be angry with him. He always creates so much goodwill. I wish there was more of Paddington in me."[35]

---

[35] Tyzack, Anna. "Olympics 2012: Darkest Peru to the London Games." www.telegraph.co.uk.

The small bear that Michael Bond purchased at Selfridge's in 1956 now resides part-time with Michael and part-time with Brenda, the wife for whom it was bought. The joint custody arrangement has worked well. The original Paddington occasionally accompanies Michael on his beloved trips to Paris, but do not worry that he will end up in the lost and found area of a train station; there is attached to his collar a label bearing his name and address, and he sticks very close to Michael since he is quite a private bear, in stark contrast to his character in the storybooks. He much prefers a quiet existence, away from the limelight, and never in a place where "things" are likely to happen!

In his autobiography, Michael recalls visiting his former home in Reading and reminiscing of his time as a child growing up there. His thoughts turned to his parents, both having passed away by this time. With some regret, he remarked, "I could have thanked them for my childhood, which I never did. It is the kind of thing one always leaves until it's too late. Most of all, I could have thanked them for giving me a love of books and the gift of being able to read them at an early age, for it brought me not only immeasurable pleasure but my livelihood too."[36] No doubt, Bond's parents had an inkling of his gratitude, in that intuitive way that parents have, and perhaps would even add that he had more than "made up" for leaving school at such an early age. By any standards, he has mastered his craft and brought untold joy to the world.

---

[36] Bond, p. 275.

It is estimated that more than 35 million Paddington books have been sold worldwide. The stories have been translated into more than forty languages. Plush Paddington toys and other merchandise continue to be sold on a global scale. But at the heart of the sales and merchandising, there lies this furry, friendly figment of Michael Bond's imagination who has captivated audiences across continents and generations and who will likely continue this noble work for many years to come. A mere glance at the image created by Peggy Fortnum so many years ago will at once warm the heart, inspire the soul, and challenge the mind. Paddington Bear, the little guy who never backs down or shrinks away from a challenge, will forever remain the champion of adventure, lost causes, and optimism. Who can help but be inspired and encouraged by such a spirit?

Works Cited

Ash, Russell. *The Life and Times of Paddington Bear*. London: Pavilion Books Limited, 1988. Print.

Ben Whishaw Cast as New Paddington Bear. 18 July 2014. 25 July 2014. <www.bbc.com/news/entertainment>.

Bond, Michael. *Bears and Forebears: A Life So Far*. London: HarperCollins, 1996. Book.

Clarkson, Shirley. *Bearly Believable: My Part in the Paddington Bear Story*. London: Harriman House, 2008. Print.

Commire, Anne. "Michael Bond." *Something about the Author, Volume 58*. Detroit: Gale Research Inc., 1990. 14-29. Book.

Hunt, Caroline, ed. *Dictionary of Literary Biography, British Children's Writers since 1960*. Vol. 161. Detroit: Gale Research, 1996. Book.

Paddington. n.d. 28 July 2014. <www.imdb.com>.

Paddington Bear Set for Big Screen Makeover. 10 May 2012. website. 25 July 2014. <www.bbc.com/news/entertainment-arts/>.

Thomas Michael Bond. n.d. 28 July 2014. <www.biography.jrank.org>.

Tyzack, Anna. "Olympics 2012: Darkest Peru to the London Games." 30 April 2012. *www.telegraph.co.uk/lifestyle.* website. 18 July 2014.

www.paddington.com. n.d. web. 24 May 2014.

Printed in Great Britain
by Amazon.co.uk, Ltd.,
Marston Gate.